CLASS 156 DMUs

Rich Mackin

AMBERLEY

First published 2017

Amberley Publishing
The Hill, Stroud
Gloucestershire, GL5 4EP

www.amberley-books.com

Copyright © Rich Mackin, 2017

The right of Rich Mackin to be identified as
the Author of this work has been asserted in
accordance with the Copyright, Designs and
Patents Act 1988.

ISBN 978 1 4456 7141 3 (print)
ISBN 978 1 4456 7142 0 (ebook)

British Library Cataloguing in Publication Data.
A catalogue record for this book is available from
the British Library.

Origination by Amberley Publishing.
Printed in the UK.

Foreword

Ordered by British Rail in November 1985 and delivered by Metro-Cammell between 1987 and 1989, the 114-strong Class 156 fleet has enjoyed a wide and varied career across the UK, from Scotland to East Anglia and South Wales. Thirty years after the first unit emerged from Washwood Heath on a test run to Banbury, the fleet remains at full strength with Scotrail, Northern, East Midlands Trains and Greater Anglia. Initially part of the 'Sprinter' family of Diesel Multiple Units, the Class 156s soon gained 'Super Sprinter' branding to signify their use on longer-distance services. At the end of the 1980s they replaced a number of older DMUs and locomotive-hauled trains on regional services, as well as longer-distance services with lower passenger numbers. Popular with drivers and passengers, they can be found on similar services today and look set to have a future well into the 2020s.

This book aims to look at the current operations of these workhorses during their operations on the privatised railway network. Most of the Class is covered, from Scotland to East Anglia. With the Class undergoing further refurbishments to enable them to work beyond 2019 (including fitting accessible toilets and passenger information displays), these hard-working DMUs will continue to enjoy a life of carrying passengers around the UK's rail network.

The doyen Class 156, No. 156401, is ready to form a late afternoon East Midlands Trains service from Lincoln's Platform 4 on 28 September 2013, bound for Nottingham. No. 156401 emerged from Metro Cammell's Washwood Heath works, in Birmingham, on 10 November 1987. After initially running to Tyseley, it performed two test runs to Banbury before returning to Washwood Heath.

National Express East Anglia's No. 156402 is far from home at Doncaster, visiting Wabtec for a mechanical overhaul. Advertising Norwich's Chapelfield shopping centre, it basks in the low winter sun at Doncaster West Yard on 10 February 2008. This unit was used for British Rail's press launch for the Class on 14 January 1987 at Norwich station, before embarking on a number of demonstration runs around Scotland.

A closer look at the vinyls advertising Norwich's Chapelfield shopping centre.

No. 156402 would later lose the colourful Chapelfield advertising livery in favour of Abellio Greater Anglia's more austere plain white livery. Looking immaculate, it awaits its next duty at Norwich on 10 February 2008. On 26 January 1988, this worked an Inverness–Wick service, becoming the first Class 156 to carry fare-paying passengers.

East Midlands Trains' fleet of Class 156s is based at Derby Etches Park – a move which took place when the former Central Trains franchise was split, with East Midlands local services forming a new franchise alongside inter-city services operating out of London St Pancras. EMT's small Class 156 fleet operates alongside Class 153s on services through Derbyshire, Nottinghamshire and Lincolnshire, and as far east as Skegness. No. 156403 was displayed at an open day at Etches Park on 13 September 2014. EMT's blue, yellow and red livery originated on the Class 450 EMUs of sister company South West Trains, and is used to differentiate stock intended for local services from the franchise's long-distance HSTs and Class 158s.

East Midlands Trains' No. 156406 arrives at Lincoln with a service from Nottingham on 22 August 2009, passing the level crossing at the city's High Street.

With the day's light fading on 4 October 2008, East Midlands Trains' No. 156410 is ready to form a service to Spalding at Peterborough. Working interchangeably with Class 153s (which usually work in pairs), this is one of the southernmost stations currently served by Class 156s.

A former Class 156-operated service now consigned to history was a lengthy service between Skegness and Crewe, which was operated by Central Trains. Prone to cancellations and delays, the service was split with separate portions between Crewe and Derby, and Nottingham and Skegness. On 31 August 2005, No. 156411 pauses at Derby's Platform 5 with a service from Skegness. It will reverse here before journeying onward to Crewe via Uttoxeter and Stoke-on-Trent.

East Midlands Trains' No. 156413 arrives at Nottingham with a service from Mansfield Woodhouse on 7 April 2017. EMT's Class 156 fleet can often be found covering destinations to and from Nottingham, visiting the nearby Eastcroft depot for maintenance.

East Midlands Trains' No. 156414 shows off a clean and well-maintained interior, despite a day's service. The unit has just terminated at Doncaster with a service from Sleaford on 7 April 2017. The unit is kept in good working order by the staff at Etches Park.

No. 156414 approaches Lincoln with 2K62, the 17:56 Sleaford–Doncaster, on 7 April 2017. This is one of the longest services operated by EMT's Class 156 fleet, taking around an hour and a half.

Abellio Greater Anglia's No. 156419 still wears the grey and white livery of previous operator National Express East Anglia at Norwich. It is seen on 22 March 2013 after working a service from Great Yarmouth. Greater Anglia's small Class 156 fleet is used on local services in Norfolk and Suffolk, and is based at Norwich Crown Point depot. Class 90 No. 90003 is parked alongside, also wearing the previous operator's colours.

Newton Heath-allocated No. 156420 is a long way from home as it arrives at Middlesbrough with a service from Whitby on 3 June 2013. No. 156420 has since moved to Allerton with the rest of the Class 156s that were previously allocated to the Manchester depot.

No. 156420 leaves Darlington with the 2D26 service to Whitby on the afternoon of 28 April 2013. While services to the coastal town normally start and terminate at Middlesbrough, on Sundays they extend farther afield to Darlington and Bishop Auckland.

A close-up of the *La'al Ratty, Ravenglass & Eskdale Railway* name applied to No. 156420. Northern Rail have named a number of their Class 156s, usually in the form of a vinyl sticker.

First North Western's No. 156420 rests at Manchester Piccadilly on 27 June 2004. FNW began painting their fleet in First Group's corporate colours shortly before losing this franchise to Serco/Abellio's Northern.

Class 156 DMUs

Wearing the somewhat garish livery of East Anglia operator 'One', No. 156422 is stabled alongside Ipswich station on the afternoon of 13 July 2006. Class 156s replaced older Class 150 Sprinter DMUs in 2005, forming a small fleet based at Norwich Crown Point in a direct swap with Central Trains.

At Carlisle on 25 September 2004, No. 156426 is wearing the long-defunct colours of North West Regional Railways. The livery was applied to a handful of Class 156s in the final years of British Rail, when passenger operations were split into small 'Train Operating Units' in readiness for privatisation. By 2004 NWRR's area had become First North Western, and a couple of months later the franchise would form part of Serco/Abellio-operated Northern Rail.

First Group-liveried No. 156428 rests at the buffers at Manchester Piccadilly alongside Class 150 'Sprinter' No. 150149 on 8 July 2007. Both Classes are a common sight around the North West, and Manchester's Newton Heath depot maintained two large fleets at the time this photograph was taken. The Class 156s have since relocated to Allerton in Liverpool.

A recently repainted No. 156429 awaits its next working at Darlington on the afternoon of 7 June 2015. Penned in by a Class 142, it will form a later service to Saltburn.

Scotrail's No. 156430 spends the day spare at Glasgow Central on 1 August 2017. The Super Sprinter is on standby should any units fail in service during the day.

Consecutively numbered No. 156430 and No. 156431 rest at Glasgow Central on 1 August 2017.

A pair of Scotrail Class 156s await their next duties at Glasgow Central on 1 August 2017. They are joined by a pair of Class 314s, which are still wearing the obsolete SPT Rail livery that used to be a common sight in and around the city.

Scotrail's No. 156432 rests between duties at Newcastle Central before forming a service to Glasgow. On 3 October 1988, No. 156432 was the first Class 156 to work from Scotland to England when it formed the 15:48 Glasgow–Newcastle service, with a ceremony being held at Glasgow prior to departure.

No. 156432 has just arrived at Glasgow Central with a service from Edinburgh (via Shotts) on 1 August 2017, and is seen resting alongside No. 156509.

No. 156432 forms a service to Edinburgh Waverley at Glasgow Central, joined by No. 156509.

Scotrail's No. 156432 leaves Belshill with a service to Edinburgh on 1 August 2017. Class 156s are the staple motive power on services between Glasgow and Edinburgh via Shotts, forming an hourly service. This is set to change in 2019 when the route is electrified.

Scotrail's No. 156433, named *The Kilmarnock Edition*, was the first unit to carry the second version of SPT Rail livery. This replaced the orange and black livery seen on many DMUs and EMUs since the 1980s. No. 156433 wore this unique version of the livery until it was repainted into the Saltire livery some years later. It is seen here at Newcastle on 21 April 2005. Subsequent SPT Rail repaints sported a revised version of this livery.

A closer look at *The Kilmnarnock Edition* nameplates applied to No. 156433. Unusually for a multiple unit, a cast nameplate has been fitted rather than the vinyl names typically applied. Named after a collection of poems by Robert Burns, it carried the plates until it lost SPT Rail livery.

In recently applied Saltire livery, Scotrail's No. 156434 visits Newcastle Central on 26 March 2010. By this time, both the First Scotrail and SPT Rail liveries were giving way to the franchise-specified livery.

With the complex approach to Glasgow Central as a backdrop, No. 156435 approaches the Scottish city with a service from East Kilbride on 1 August 2017, passing Class 314 No. 314214 (on a Cathcart circle working). This shows the complex array of track and signalling outside the busy terminus.

Sunlight shines through the roof of Glasgow Central as No. 156435 arrives at the Scottish terminus, where it is surrounded by Scotrail EMUs.

The driver of Scotrail's No. 156434 takes a break from the cab at Glasgow Central before working 2J16 to East Kilbride on 1 August 2017.

Passengers disembark No. 156436 at Glasgow Central, having arrived on a service from East Kilbride.

Scotrail's Class 156 fleet regularly operate to Carlisle and across the Tyne Valley route to Newcastle (crewed by Northern between the English cities). Most of the fleet now carries the Saltire livery, branded 'Scotrail – Scotland's railway' in both English and Gaelic. At Newcastle, No. 156437 has formed a service from Glasgow Central, via Kilmarnock and Carlisle, on 10 August 2015.

Northern's No. 156438 arrives at Newcastle with a service from Carlisle after heavy snowfall on 28 November 2010. As it arrives an East Coast Class 91 bound for London propels a Mk 4 rake south over the King Edward Bridge.

Northern's No. 156438 was named *Timothy Hackworth* in a ceremony at Darlington on 17 March 2012. The railway pioneer was represented by children from Timothy Hackworth School, Shildon, who wore traditional Victorian clothing. The unit was named by Richard Allan (left), Northern's area director for the North East, along with Jane Hackworth-Young, Timothy's great-great granddaughter.

In heavy snow, No. 156438 leaves Darlington with a service to Middlesbrough on 21 February 2010. No doubt the passengers were grateful for the warmth of a Class 156 in preference to the draughty Class 142s, which normally ply their trade on Tees Valley services!

Northern's No. 156438 arrives at Darlington's Platform 2 with a service from Saltburn on an overcast 23 February 2014.

Scotrail's No. 156439 leaves Newcastle with a service for Glasgow Central on 23 January 2017. The unit is leaving the East Coast Main Line for the city's High Level Bridge before it heads toward Hexham and Carlisle.

Allerton-based No. 156440 *George Bradshaw* visited the North East on 23 March 2017, arriving at Newcastle with a service from Nunthorpe. The unit is named for the nineteenth-century publisher of railway travel guides recently re-popularised by the *Great British Railway Journeys* television series.

Northern's No. 156441 was still wearing First Group livery when it was photographed at York on 17 March 2007. A subsequent reshuffle of Northern's fleet saw the Class 156s based at Heaton and Newton Heath, banishing the Super Sprinters from the York and Leeds area.

While wearing Northern Spirit livery, No. 156443 could always be easily distinguished from Arriva's other Class 156s by the yellow warning panel extending around to the cab sides.

Northern often stables a spare Class 156 at Darlington, either in the bay platforms or on the bi-directional single line adjacent to Platform 1. The latter option has been chosen for No. 156443 on 25 March 2012.

Northern's No. 156443 leaves Middlesbrough with a service to Nunthorpe on 24 February 2017. The unit is wearing the short-lived 'We Are Northern' branding that was carried by a handful of Class 156s, which is now being replaced by the new white and purple livery seen later in this book.

The transformation of the Arriva-operated franchise is evident at Darlington with both No. 156443 and No. 156454 wearing the new livery following refurbishment. The livery was rapidly applied to the fleet during the summer of 2017.

The BREL P3-10 bogie houses the Gmeinder Final Drive that connects the Voith hydraulic transmission to the Cummins diesel engine that powers every Class 156 vehicle. One bogie under each vehicle is powered, at the inner end of each vehicle.

A BREL BT38 bogie sits under the outer end of each Class 156 vehicle. Externally similar to the P3-10, it lacks any kind of drive system.

Northern's Class 156s regularly operate services around the Cumbria coast, and are currently sharing these duties with Class 37s. Before the locomotive-hauled services were introduced, No. 156444 waits at Carlisle with a service to Barrow-in-Furness on 27 April 2013.

Northern's No. 156444 calls at Middlesbrough, and is seen sharing the Teesside station with 'Pacer' No. 142025. While the destination blind shows 'Saltburn', the unit's journey began at the seaside town and will end in Darlington.

Northern's No. 156444 leaves Middlesbrough with a Saltburn–Darlington service on 3 April 2013.

No. 156444 arrives at Newcastle with the local Metrocentre shuttle service on 6 March 2005. This is one of Northern's shortest services, covering a grand total of just under 3½ miles.

Northern's No. 156444 leaves Newcastle with a service to Middlesbrough (via Sunderland, Hartlepool and Stockton) on 9 August 2008.

In SPT Rail livery, Scotrail's No. 156445 waits to depart Carlisle on 7 July 2007. The north-facing bay platforms are typically used for services to Glasgow Central via Kilmarnock.

Scotrail's No. 156445 undergoes a clean and a coolant top-up at Glasgow Queen Street on 24 May 2017.

No. 156448 arrives at Newcastle with a terminating service from Morpeth on 23 April 2012. Class 156s often feature on this stopping service.

Advertising the local attraction of Hadrian's Wall, No. 156448 rests at Newcastle on 26 March 2012. The unit will later travel more or less along the route of the ancient Roman defensive wall, ending at Carlisle.

Northern's No. 156448 calls at Shildon with a Saltburn–Bishop Auckland service on 21 September 2008.

No. 156448 advertised 'Hadrian's Wall Country', showing off the scenery between Newcastle and Carlisle.

No. 156449 is still wearing First Group livery when seen arriving at Glasgow Central on 24 May 2017, some years after the livery was rendered obsolete.

Still wearing the old First Group livery, Scotrail's No. 156449 rests at a wet Newcastle on 23 April 2012. No sooner had First Group livery been applied to the fleet than the decision was taken to adopt a franchise-independent livery that the Scotrail fleet would carry irrespective of the operating company.

Scotrail's No. 156450 rests at Glasgow Central after forming a service from Edinburgh Waverley via Shotts. Class 156s are the principle traction on this route, taking a scenic but slow route between Scotland's two largest cities.

Northern's No. 156451 is the assigned spare at Darlington on the morning of 17 October 2010.

Northern's No. 156451 leaves Darlington with a Saltburn service on 18 February 2006. Northern were very slow to adopt a corporate livery, trialling several colour schemes on Class 156s in 2005, with this being one of them.

Finally wearing Northern's corporate livery, No. 156451 leaves Darlington with an evening service to Saltburn on a sunny 28 May 2010.

Long after Northern chose their final colour scheme, No. 156451 is seen still wearing its trial livery when leaving Newcastle with a service to Middlesbrough on 15 March 2008.

First Group livery lingers on with No. 156453, which is seen leaving Carlisle on 24 May 2017 with a service to Glasgow Central via Dumfries.

Scotrail's No. 156453 is very far from home when seen here at Crewe on 11 July 2006. The unit was heading to Wolverton Works for a refresh and repaint, and is seen still wearing the old livery of the National Express-operated Scotrail franchise.

Newcastle's Platform 1 is a frequent haunt for Scotrail units working to Carlisle and Newcastle. On 29 February 2016, No. 156453 waits to form the 13:23 departure to the Scottish city.

On a sunny early autumn evening on 6 October 2003, Arriva Trains Northern's No. 156454 leaves Darlington on a Bishop Auckland–Saltburn service. Arriva never applied their corporate livery to any Class 156s, retaining instead the Northern Spirit livery applied in the late 1990s.

Northern's No. 156454 rests between services at Darlington on 13 March 2016. This unit has been fitted with a large accessible toilet, which is identifiable by the large blank space and the small window adjacent to the nearest passenger door. All Class 156s are receiving similar modifications to allow them to remain in service after 31 December 2019.

No. 156454 calls at Metrocentre with a service to Hexham, 27 February 2011.

Northern's No. 156464 forms a service from the Metrocentre at Newcastle on 16 July 2009.

First North Western's No. 156455 arrives at Manchester Piccadilly on 27 June 2004. This unit is still wearing the North West Regional Railways livery, which added a green stripe to the livery applied to stock working regional services between 1990 and 1996.

Scotrail's First Group-liveried No. 156456 leaves Glasgow Central with a service to Carlisle on 1 August 2017. The journey to the English border city is a long one, travelling via Kilmarnock rather than the direct route via the West Coast Main Line.

The old and current liveries of Scotrail meet at Glasgow Central on No. 156458 and No. 156442 on 24 May 2017. No. 156442 is about to form a service to Edinburgh via Shotts.

Other than some worn paint on the cab, the old First Group livery on No. 156458 is in good condition when seen at Glasgow Central on 24 May 2017, despite the livery having been applied a number of years ago.

No. 156461 wore what would become Northern's final livery when it was seen leaving Doncaster on 3 July 2005 with a service to Sheffield. Applied to the base dark blue of First North Western, the livery would be further tweaked with a lighter shade of blue before being applied across the fleet. Even that would later change when the angled upswept stripes were replaced with a curved design.

Vinyls later applied to No. 156461 advertise the Ravenglass & Eskdale Railway, showing scenes of the popular Cumbrian tourist attraction.

No. 156461 was one of the first Northern Class 156s to carry an advertising livery, with the upswept mauve stripe carrying vinyls. The unit is seen at a very gloomy Darlington on 23 September 2006.

Another look at No. 156461's Ravenglass & Eskdale Railway advertising livery.

The interior of No. 156462, showing the spacious Class 156 interior with relatively low-backed seats and a large number of seating bays around tables. The scrolling LED destination display is visible at the far end.

Still wearing the old First Group livery, No. 156462's crew changes ends at Anniesland on 1 August 2017. Class 156s operate a regular service throughout the day on the short route to Glasgow Queen Street via Maryhill.

The new and old Northern liveries meet at Darlington on 25 June 2017, with No. 156463 wearing the livery of the new Arriva-operated franchise, while sibling No. 156438 still carries the old Serco/Abellio livery. At the time of writing, the Class 156s are rapidly being vinyled in the new livery.

Northern's No. 156463 rests on the single line adjacent to Darlington's Platform 1 on 22 January 2012. It is not uncommon for a spare unit to be stabled here.

Renewed after an internal and external refresh, No. 156463 is wearing the livery of the new Arriva-operated Northern franchise. Whether or not the primarily white-based livery remains clean over time remains to be seen!

Northern's No. 156463 leaves a sunny Middlesbrough with a service to Saltburn on 3 June 2016.

The early morning sun's long shadows have all but covered Northern's No. 156463 at Middlesbrough on 13 May 2005. The unit, still wearing Northern Spirit livery, is forming the day's first service to Whitby. A large volume of children travelling to and from school at Whitby means that Northern will use a Class 156 on these services.

A pair of Class 156s occupy the platforms at Middlesbrough on 25 September 2015, namely No. 156464 and No. 156491. The latter is forming a service to Whitby, while the former is on a Newcastle–Nunthorpe service.

The third livery trialled by Northern in 2005 involved a primarily white colour scheme, which is seen applied to No. 156464. The Newton Heath-based unit is seen at Heaton depot on 14 September 2008.

The name and advertising livery applied to Northern's No. 156464 indicate that it is far from home at Middlesbrough on 25 September 2015. Named *Lancashire DalesRail*, it is advertising scenic walks and education/conservation projects in Lancashire.

Northern's No. 156466 rests at Manchester Piccadilly on 13 April 2012. Class 156s have recently been cascaded from a number of services in and around Manchester by Class 319s following the completion of electrification to Liverpool.

Spring sunshine casts shadows over First Scotrail's No. 156467 at Newcastle on 29 April 2008.

Still in Northern Spirit livery with small 'Northern' branding, No. 156468 leaves Newcastle on 4 July 2007.

No. 156469 *The Royal Northumberland Fusiliers (The Fighting 5th)* leaves Carlisle with 2M34, the Newcastle–Whitehaven service, on 24 May 2017 after reversing at the English border city. This is the only service from Newcastle that ventures further into Cumbria beyond Carlisle, where most services terminate.

With an advertising livery based on the earlier version of Northern's livery with angled stripes, No. 156469 prepares for an overnight stay at Darlington on 23 September 2006. The unit had been working extra services between Darlington and Bishop Auckland in connection with an ACoRP community rail weekend, which would resume in the morning.

No. 156469 leaves Middlesbrough with a service to Hexham on 4 September 2012. This is one of Northern's longer services, usually taking around two hours and fifteen minutes.

Northern's No. 156470 calls at Metrocentre with a service to Carlisle on 29 April 2008.

Later transferring to East Midlands Trains, a recently repainted No. 156470 leaves Derby with a service from Matlock to Newark Castle on 13 September 2014.

No. 156470 prepares to leave Lincoln with a service to Newark North Gate on 7 April 2017.

Former Northern Spirit unit No. 156471 calls at Doncaster with a service to Hull on 3 July 2005.

No. 156471 approaches Middlesbrough with a service from Whitby on 4 September 2012. A single unit usually covers the Whitby branch service on any given day, setting off from Darlington early in the morning and returning there at the end of the day.

Refurbished No. 156471 leaves Newcastle with a service to Nunthorpe on 27 March 2017. This is one of the first units to wear the new Arriva-operated Northern livery, which was applied after the unit was fitted with an accessible toilet and an LED destination display. By the summer of 2017 this new livery was being rapidly rolled out across Northern's fleet.

No. 156472 arrives at Newcastle with a local service on 7 May 2005.

At Newcastle, Northern's No. 156473 (still in Northern Spirit livery) has arrived with a service from Carlisle.

Scotrail's No. 156474 is ready to leave Glasgow Central with a service to Kilmarnock on 25 February 2006.

Northern's No. 156475 is seen at Carlisle on the afternoon of 27 April 2013 with a service across the Tyne Valley to Newcastle.

Former Northern Spirit unit No. 156476 is seen on the morning of 3 July 2005 at Doncaster with a service to Hull.

No. 156475 leaves a sunny Darlington on the afternoon of 6 September 2015 with a Bishop Auckland–Saltburn service.

No. 156475 passes the level crossing at the end of Cargo Fleet Road, Middlesbrough, with the 2D40 service from the Teesside town to Whitby on 24 February 2017.

Scotrail's No. 156476 rests at Glasgow Central after arriving with a service from Kilmarnock on 26 February 2005. Though operated by First Group, the unit is still wearing the livery of the previous National Express-held franchise. On 6 November 1989, No. 156476 was involved in a collision at Huddersfield with Pacer No. 141104 and spent several months under repair at Doncaster while the Class 141 was withdrawn.

Scotrail's No. 156477, one of a number of Class 156s still in First Group livery some years after the Saltire livery was introduced, awaits its next duty at Glasgow Queen Street.

No. 156478 came close to being the first Class 156 to be withdrawn after incurring severe flood damage near Mauchline in December 2014. The unit was written off due to a six-figure repair bill, and was sold to Kilmarnock-based Brodie Engineering, who repaired it. It returned to service in October 2016, with Brodie Engineering leasing it directly to Scotrail. This unlikely survivor is seen at Newcastle on 27 March 2017.

No. 156478 shows off the English and Gaelic versions of the Scotrail branding applied across their entire fleet.

Brodie Engineering-owned No. 156478 is seen at Glasgow Central on 24 May 2017, where it was working the regular shuttle service to Anniesland.

Recently returned to service, Brodie Engineering-owned No. 156478 rests at Glasgow Central on 1 August 2017.

No. 156479 arrives at Carlisle with a service from Newcastle on 27 April 2013.

Sundays on the Whitby branch only see services during the summer months, but this is expected to change in 2017 with the welcome return of a year-round service. On 5 May 2013, No. 156479 calls at Grosmont with the 2D02 Bishop Auckland–Whitby service. This is an especially long working for Class 156s in the North East, with a total journey time of two hours and twenty-four minutes between twenty-eight stations. These are among the few North East services operated exclusively by the Class, with Pacers being a rare sight on the Esk Valley line.

A bright winter's day casts a pattern of shadows over Northern's No. 156479 at Newcastle as it forms a service to Carlisle on 30 January 2015.

Northern's No. 156479 passes Pelaw with a Newcastle–Middlesbrough service via the Durham coast on 28 February 2014.

Many years after the Northern Spirit branding disappeared (after parent company MTL was acquired by Arriva), their turquoise and green livery could still be found on Class 156s. Northern's No. 156480 was one such unit, which is seen at Newcastle on 3 May 2008.

Northern's No. 156480 eventually gained the operator's blue, mauve and white livery, and is seen here at Newcastle on 7 April 2012.

Northern's No. 156481 and Scotrail's No. 156445 share Platform 1 at Newcastle on 29 February 2012, providing a rare opportunity to compare two different operators' Class 156s side by side.

With a thin plume of exhaust, No. 156481 occupies Platform 12 at Newcastle with a service to Carlisle on 16 July 2009.

Northern's No. 156481 approaches Newcastle with a service from Carlisle on 30 January 2015.

No. 156482 calls at Doncaster with a Hull–Sheffield service on 3 July 2005. Since Neville Hill lost its allocation of Class 156s, these units are now a rare sight in much of Yorkshire.

Northern's No. 156482 arrives at Newcastle with a local service on 29 February 2016. This unit has been fitted with an LED destination display, which can prove difficult to capture on photographs due to a 'strobe' effect that is invisible to the naked eye.

With a covering of snow, No. 156484 and No. 142015 bask in winter sunshine at Darlington on 5 February 2012.

No. 156484 leaves a snowy Darlington on 5 February 2012 with a service to Saltburn, sporting Leeds–Settle–Carlisle advertising livery. Despite the livery, the route in question is usually operated by Class 158s.

Northern's No. 156484 reaches out from the shadows of Darlington's Victorian train shed on 13 March 2010.

Northern's No. 156484 advertises the scenic Leeds–Settle–Carlisle line, showing some of the popular route's sights. The livery features two separate graphics, which are shown on each side of both vehicles.

Ribblehead Viaduct, one of the scenic highlights of the Leeds–Settle–Carlisle route, is highlighted on No. 156484's advertising livery.

At Newcastle, Northern's No. 156486 is ready to depart with a service to Carlisle on 5 November 2006.

No. 156486 leaves Newcastle with a service to Morpeth on 23 January 2017, illuminated by low winter sun.

With a light dusting of snow, Arriva Trains Northern's No. 156488 was captured at Darlington with a service to Saltburn on 28 January 2004.

No. 156489 passes Darlington with an empty stock movement from Heaton on 23 February 2014, passing an engineer's train.

Northern's No. 156489 calls at Skipton with a Leeds–Carlisle service on 1 July 2006. Class 156s are rare on this route, with Northern preferring to use Class 158s on the scenic journey through the Yorkshire dales.

Northern's No. 156490 is carrying advertising livery for York's National Railway Museum when seen at Darlington on 8 December 2013. Will one of these long-serving units find a home at the museum when they eventually retire?

Northern's No. 156490, still wearing Northern Spirit livery, rests at Darlington between services to and from Saltburn on 11 November 2007.

In wet weather, Northern's No. 156490 sits at Newcastle's Platform 1 on 5 May 2012 with another unit parked behind it.

A close look at the National Railway Museum advertising vinyls applied to No. 156490.

A record-breaking steam locomotive is given due prominence on No. 156490's National Railway Museum advertising vinyls, drawing visitors to the ever-popular museum.

Scotrail's No. 156492 occupies Platform 1 at Newcastle on 1 May 2015. While there are only a handful of daily services to Glasgow Central, their Class 156s are a regular sight at the English city.

Scotrail's No. 156493 leaves Edinburgh with a service to Newcraighall on 14 July 2006. Since the line reopened to Tweedback, Class 158s have taken over services.

Later on 14 July 2006, No. 156493 has Class 170 Turbostar No. 170422 for company at Edinburgh Waverley.

Scotrail and Northern meet at the Metrocentre on 7 July 2008. The small two-platform station opened in the 1980s to serve what was once the largest shopping and leisure centre in the UK. Scotrail's No. 156494 calls with a service to Newcastle, while Northern's No. 156448 has just terminated with a shuttle service from the city. Metrocentre used to see services from as far afield as Saltburn, which were gradually cut back to Darlington, then to Newcastle, under the previous Arriva-operated North-East franchise.

In the British Rail carmine and cream-inspired livery of SPT Rail, Scotrail's No. 156495 awaits its next duty at Glasgow Central on 4 July 2007.

Scotrail's No. 156495 prepares to work a service to East Kilbride from Glasgow Central on 1 August 2017. Class 156s operate a half-hourly service on the 11½-mile route throughout the day.

In a murky Glasgow Queen Street, No. 156496 forms a service to Anniesland on 1 August 2017. The station is due to undergo redevelopment, which includes replacing the dated concourse. The station is already electrified in anticipation of Class 385 EMUs entering service between here and Edinburgh.

The evidence of the old First Group livery is apparent on No. 156496, showing the older Scotrail branding with the flying 'F' logo removed, as the franchise passed to Abellio in 2015.

The Scotrail franchise holder is allowed to place a small piece of corporate branding on their rolling stock – a far cry from the many and varied liveries that privatisation offered. This is usually in the form of a vinyl sticker applied to each door, stating that the service is operated by Abellio. Should the franchise change hands in future, that operator will replace the discrete branding with their own.

Both in the old First Group livery, No. 156496 and No. 156447 face off at Glasgow Queen Street on 1 August 2017.

Scotrail's No. 156496 rests at Glasgow Queen Street after working a service from Anniesland. From Queen Street, Class 156s are usually seen on the local shuttle working to Anniesland and on long-distance services to Mallaig, Fort William and Oban.

The lines of the obsolete First Group livery are evident on No. 156496 at Glasgow Queen Street. Applied during the previous Scotrail franchise, the livery was replaced by the Transport Scotland-specified Saltire livery almost as soon as the National Express Scotrail livery was removed from the fleet.

On 29 August 2002 Arriva's No. 156497 reaches journey's end at Darlington with an evening service from Saltburn.

A guard prepares for departure at Darlington on 12 April 2007 as No. 156497 forms a Saltburn–Bishop Auckland service. Even though Northern took over local services in the region in 2004, the unit is still in Northern Spirit livery – a commonplace sight even in 2007.

Arriva Trains Northern's No. 156498 arrives at Newcastle on 9 April 2004. Arriva only painted a handful of units while they held the North East franchise, with all their Class 156s retaining the old Northern Spirit livery applied in 1998/99.

East Midlands Trains' No. 156498 catches the last of the day's sun at Lincoln while waiting with a service to Peterborough on 28 September 2013. This unit transferred from Northern the year before.

Scotrail's No. 156499 lurks inside Glasgow Queen Street on a particularly murky day, with the dark blue livery doing little to help the unit stand out from its surroundings on 24 May 2017.

De-branded No. 156500 sits at Newcastle on 19 December 2008. The SPT Rail branding has been removed, and the livery itself will soon give way to Scotrail's Saltire livery.

The guard of Scotrail's No. 156501 watches the doors at Carlisle's Platform 1 before the unit heads north on 16 July 2011. Class 156s are unusual visitors to this side of the station, instead usually using the higher-numbered platforms.

Matching SPT Rail pair No. 156502 and No. 156503 await their next duties at Glasgow Central on 25 February 2006.

Scotrail's No. 156502 arrives at Newcastle with a service from Glasgow Central on 31 May 2010.

Scotrail's No. 156503 awaits its next duty at Glasgow Central on 24 May 2017. The unit, along with the rest of Scotrail's 'Super Sprinter' fleet, is maintained a short distance away at Corkerhill depot.

Edinburgh Waverley's roof casts shadows over SPT Rail-liveried No. 156504 on 14 July 2006. The unit has just arrived with a service from Newcraighall.

The scrolling LED display on Scotrail's No. 156505 shows Glasgow Central as the destination as the Class 156 awaits passengers at Carlisle on 27 April 2013.

National Express-operated Scotrail's No. 156505 calls at Haymarket with a service to Edinburgh Waverley on 29 February 2004.

No. 156505 departs Metrocentre with a Newcastle–Glasgow Central service on 15 November 2010.

Scotrail's No. 156506 rests at Newcastle's Platform 1 on 26 March 2012. The car park on the right sits on the former site of the once-electrified suburban platforms.

No. 156506 forms a service to East Kilbride at Glasgow Central on 1 August 2017. Class 156s are the principal diesel motive power at the Scottish terminus, though Class 158s can make an appearance. From here they operate to such destinations as Edinburgh, Kilmarnock, Carlisle, Newcastle, East Kilbride and Barrhead.

Wearing the Saltire livery of Scotrail, No. 156507 occupies Newcastle's Platform 1 on 26 June 2013. The blue and white livery marked a change in rail franchise liveries, with the livery remaining the same irrespective of the operating company. Small 'Operated by First' stickers are just visible on the passenger doors – the extent of corporate branding permitted on the new livery. A similar model is now being rolled out across the remaining franchises.

Scotrail's Strathclyde Partnership for Transport-liveried No. 156508 is seen at Newcastle on 3 May 2008 after working a service from Glasgow Central.

Scotrail's No. 156508 waits to form a service to Barrhead at Glasgow Central alongside classmate No. 156430 on 1 August 2017. The two different typefaces applied to Scotrail units are evident here, with No. 156508 carrying the later style.

A freshly repainted No. 156508 rests at Glasgow Central. The immaculate yellow warning panel and obstacle deflector are evidence of the livery applied after the unit was fitted with a disabled toilet.

Nos 156430, 156508 and 156509 rest at Glasgow Central on 1 August 2017.

Scotrail's Saltire-liveried No. 156509 lurks in the shadows of Newcastle's Platform 1 on 30 January 2015, where it is illuminated by a thin sliver of winter sun.

With EWS's No. 67023 for company, No. 156513 visits Newcastle on 9 August 2008. The SPT Rail branding has been removed after Strathclyde Passenger Transport Executive became Strathclyde Partnership for Transport in 2006, whereupon it lost its legal powers concerning rail franchising.

Scotrail's No. 156513 visits Newcastle on 9 August 2008. The SPT Rail branding has been removed after Strathclyde Passenger Transport Executive became Strathclyde Partnership for Transport in 2006, whereupon it lost its legal powers concerning rail franchising.

A recently repainted No. 156513 leaves Glasgow Central with a service to Edinburgh. The altered window arrangement at the far end is evidence that the unit has recently been fitted with a large, accessible toilet.

SPT Rail-liveried No. 156514 rests at Newcastle after arriving with a service from Scotland on 7 May 2007. SPT's carmine and cream colour scheme has since given way to Scotrail's Saltire livery. No. 156514 was the last unit to be delivered on 28 September 1989, in an Ian Allan-sponsored press run from Washwood Heath to Corkerhill depot.